preparing for

eternity

A Catholic Handbook

for End-of-Life Concerns

_____

preparing for

eternity

A Catholic Handbook

for End-of-Life Concerns

Joseph M. Champlin

ave maria press AmP notre dame, indiana

Imprimatur:

†Most Reverend Thomas J. Costello, DD

Vicar General, Diocese of Syracuse, New York

Feast of Saints Philip and James,

May 3, 2006

Scripture texts used in this work are taken from *The New American Bible* copyright © 1991, 1986, and 1970 by the Confraternity of Christian Doctrine, Washington, DC, and are used by permission of the copyright owner. All rights reserved.

Excerpts from the English translation of the *Order of Christian Funerals* © 1989, 1985 and *Pastoral Care of the Sick* © 1982, International Committee on English in the Liturgy, Inc. All rights reserved.

Excerpts from the English translation of the Catechism of the Catholic Church for use in the United States of America Copyright © 1994, United States Catholic Conference, Inc.— Libreria Editrice Vaticana. Used with Permission.

•

Founded in 1865, Ave Maria Press is a ministry of the Indiana Province of Holy Cross.

www.avemariapress.com

ISBN-10 1-59471-109-7 ISBN-13 978-1-59471-109-1

Cover and text design by David R. Scholtes

Printed and bound in the United States of America.

Contents

Introduction

Many, perhaps most, people will find the title and topic of this little book disconcerting, making them feel uncomfortable. That is because it touches upon very sensitive subjects such as our human mortality, the inevitable deterioration and sickness that precede most deaths, and our own future after this life. An unconscious denial of those issues or an expressed unwillingness to talk about them are commonplace realities in today's world.

The Terri Schiavo situation and my personal participation in a recent national teleconference on end-of-life issues sponsored by Hospice of Central New York prompted me to take some often-postponed actions. I redesigned my will, discussed with family and friends a health care proxy as well as organ donations, and developed a document detailing my funeral and burial wishes. That was a sobering but peace-giving and very satisfying experience. It seemed to complete some unfinished business that had been at least beneath the surface gnawing at me for a long time.

In addition, as a parish priest for nearly fifty years, I have witnessed literally thousands of individuals and families deeply touched by the transforming rites of the Catholic Church. I have witnessed the joy of forgiveness found in the sacrament of reconciliation, healing and strength experienced through the ritual celebrations of Pastoral Care of the Sick, and profound comfort, understanding, and hope through the Order of Christian Funerals.

The chapters of this book begin with practical examples, most of which occurred in the area where I live and have served. In addition, there are in the text some references to practices or events in New York state or Central New York. All of these are simply good illustrations, making real the points of this book.

They easily could be replicated anywhere in the United States or beyond our borders.

I pray that these pages will help you, the reader, attain this peace of mind, healing, and comfort I have experienced recently in my personal life and over five decades as a parish priest.

Father Joseph Champlin
Lent 2006

one
___

Making a Will

The young couple, married but two years and having an infant child, were returning home after a family visit in Central New York. Midway on that journey, a car crossed the median and hit them head-on with devastating effects. Both parents and child were rushed to the University Hospital in Syracuse. The father died almost immediately, the mother soon after, and Ryan, the infant son, was still hospitalized for a month although he had been strapped in the back seat of the car. Unfortunately, the young couple did not have a will. The complications because of that lack were enormous.

Both the paternal and maternal families, after many discussions, eventually agreed to work harmoniously in resolving the guardianship issue. If they had not, the state would have quickly placed Ryan in a foster home. The legal aftermath included a relatively brief six-month process after which the judge awarded guardianship of Ryan to a childless couple, his paternal aunt and her husband. However, subsequent legal battles over financial matters extended for several years, were extremely painful for all concerned, and eventually resulted in an unnecessary loss (through taxation) of substantial donations that had been made to the family.

All of that happened about two decades ago. Ryan took his guardian's surname at sixteen, later graduated from high school, and then received an appointment to the Air Force Academy.

Reasons for Postponing

His surrogate parents clearly served well as Ryan's caretakers and guardians. But the lack of a will caused needless tensions, struggles, and conflicts in his early years.

Why did his youthful parents—and why do so many contemporary people—fail to make a will? Four common reasons lead people to postpone this critical task:

1. The hectic pace of modern society

Countless individuals state that time is the most precious commodity in their lives. There are not enough moments in a day to accomplish what these persons judge they need and wish to do. Work and family duties, volunteer service, recreational activities, and any number of other tasks consume all their waking hours. Making a will may lurk in the back of their minds as a desirable goal, but it is not considered an immediate necessity and quickly yields to more pressing responsibilities.

2. A misconception of cost and complexity

As we will see, preparing a will is generally a very affordable and relatively simple project. However, many harbor a false notion that the undertaking will be costly and complicated.

3. An unwillingness to face mortality

Few people are totally comfortable speaking about death in general or their own demise in particular. Our culture reflects that uneasiness. We speak of people "passing away," not dying. We cover the dirt at a graveside with a green rug. Patients and families often deny the presence of a terminal disease. Preparing a will is a sobering, though satisfying experience. We are facing the fact that sooner or later we will die. The when and how is unknown, but our eventual death is certain. Preparing a will forces us to face our mortality. However, doing so does not hasten our death or mean that we are about to die!

4. A reluctance to resolve the difficult decisions connected with a will

There are many judgments, difficult or at least perceived as difficult, that must be made when preparing a will. Who will be named in it? How do we divide our possessions? What arrangements should we make for the children in case we die before they reach adulthood? If we haven't come to grips with these issues, why contact a lawyer?

Cost and Complexity

For an average middle class person, the lawyer's standard fee for a will ranges from $100 to $250. For some will specialists that amount may rise to $500. But for most attorneys, preparing a will is simply a service to clients and not a profit-making venture. If an individual possesses considerable wealth and significant assets (e.g., houses, collectibles, investments), the complexity and cost will probably be much greater. Persons concerned about the expense of having a will drawn up should telephone prospective lawyers with an up-front question about the approximate total cost.

In our technologically advanced world of electronic communications with ready access to fax, Internet, and e-mail, much of the will-making can be done at home or over the telephone. Only a single personal visit to the lawyer's office may be necessary to finalize the document and sign it before witnesses. It is generally a wise decision, for many reasons, to file the original, signed will in the lawyer's office for safekeeping. The attorney will provide the client with adequate copies for later distribution to appropriate people.

Major Concerns

There are usually four major concerns or issues that preoccupy persons who begin the process of making a will.

1. Future care of the children

Those making wills are most often concerned about their off-spring's welfare in the possibility that either or both parents might die prior to their children reaching independent adulthood. This includes providing financial support to a guardian or caretaker and college education expenses. These may be extremely delicate decisions. For example, why choose this person as guardian or trustee instead of someone else?

2. A preference for bloodline distribution

The divorce rate, which is close to 50 percent in the United States, has intensified this concern among people preparing their wills. People making out wills frequently express their wish that money or assets be distributed among the children or grandchildren and not to spouses of their offspring. For example, a son or daughter marries, has children, and then divorces. Many, perhaps the majority, of will-makers explicitly desire that their children (and grandchildren) receive the bequests, not their daughters-in-law or sons-in-law, due to the potential of future divorce. One does not want to encounter the inconvenience and additional cost of revising a will every time there is marital discord among descendants.

3. Equal treatment of all heirs

The will expresses in words only the final decisions of the person making the will. It does not normally explain the rationale behind them. Nevertheless, those preparing their wills are usually anxious to treat all heirs equally and fairly and to avoid their survivors having to wonder, "Why so much for this individual and less for another?"

4. The desire for unexpected elements to be understood and implemented

The opening of wills can produce many surprises. To illustrate, people may not suspect that the deceased possessed such wealth, or designated a charity as the recipient of some huge amount, or divided the inheritance unequally among the children. Moreover, a change in the original will can be a source of tension or annoyance on the part of survivors. Those making wills are anxious for their wishes to be clearly stated so that survivors will understand and precisely follow their desires.

Benefits

As I mentioned earlier, my own experience in dealing with these end-of-life issues, including the re-design of my will, was sobering, but peace-giving and very satisfying. A veteran attorney I know, after preparing many wills, has often heard reactions similar to mine: "I now feel at peace." "It was not so bad." "Now I don't have to think about these things anymore."

Quite interestingly, during the first two weeks of January, lawyers receive an unusual number of telephone inquiries, more than at any other time of the year, indicating the callers' desire to make their wills. They are fulfilling New Year's resolutions, probably made a few times before but never implemented. Of course, a will insures that what happened to Ryan in the aftermath of his parents' sudden, tragic death will not be repeated.

two

End-of-Life Issues

The Catholic wife and her Jewish spouse stood in a hospital corridor speaking quietly but anxiously with a spiritual adviser. In a nearby room the woman's eighty-year-old mother, burdened with multiple health problems, was near death. The family's physician had just informed the couple that this elderly lady would live only a few days more because of the many ailments with which she struggled. He also told them, however, that there were some extraordinary medical steps that might extend her life just a little longer. Nevertheless, her health problems were so severe that she would soon succumb to them. The decision on how to proceed belonged to the daughter.

In response to the daughter's request for guidance, the priest simply stated that they may, but need not, proceed with the extraordinary measures. In other words, it was morally correct to proceed, but there was no moral obligation to do so. That placed the daughter in a painful dilemma. She did not wish to see her mother suffer any longer, but, at the same time, dreaded the thought of being the person responsible for ending her mother's life sooner. She eventually decided not to pursue the extraordinary measures. As predicted, her mother died within a few days.

That still-tormented daughter did not feel peace until the funeral Mass. In the homily, the priest spoke about the nature of heaven in which, among other joys, there are no more tears, pain, or sorrow. Hearing those words, the woman sensed her mother's spirit thanking her for making the decision she couldn't make for herself. The daughter felt enormous relief, a burden being lifted from her shoulders. She now judged that her decision not to approve those extraordinary measures was the correct choice.

Similar incidents are replicated countless times every day in this country and beyond. The advance of medical science and health care practices has been rapid and enormous in recent decades. Consider the examples of in vitro fertilization, robotic surgeries, and laser treatments. But some of these newer practices and procedures have complex moral dimensions with which our ethical standards are trying to keep pace. This present day reality is illustrated in the subtitle of a December 2005 *Time* article that described a transplanted face operation with, "Surgeons use a donated face to reclaim a disfigured woman's life. But troubling ethical questions remain."

As in the case of that desperately ill woman in the hospital, there are no simple black and white answers to these moral challenges. However, the Church has given official statements on some of these matters. The summary of those various statements below should prove helpful to individuals and family members wrestling with such issues, including the controversial matter of artificial nutrition and hydration.

Catholic Tradition Over the Centuries

The Common Earlier Teaching

For many decades, the standard moral distinction was between ordinary and extraordinary means to preserve life. This teaching indicated that we have an obligation and *must* use ordinary means (food, water, sleep, etc.) to maintain our health. However, while we are not *obliged* to use extraordinary means (for example, complicated treatment or serious surgery), we *may* employ them to preserve or extend our health and life. In recent years this distinction between ordinary and extraordinary has shifted, as noted below.

The More Contemporary Approach

The *Catechism of the Catholic Church* (CCC) is the most current compendium of Roman Catholic teaching. Published originally in 1994 with a revised text in 1997, it contains a wealth of material on both faith and morals. Two of its paragraphs deal explicitly—albeit in a general way—with today's medical-moral issues, thus providing guidance for people like the couple in our introductory illustration. The citations deal with interrupting treatment, but are equally applicable to questions of beginning medical procedures.

2278   Discontinuing medical procedures that are burdensome, dangerous, extraordinary, or disproportionate to the expected outcome can be legitimate; it is the refusal of "over-zealous" treatment. Here one does not will to cause death; one's inability to impede it is merely accepted. The decisions should be made by the patient if he is competent and able or, if not, by those legally entitled to act for the patient, whose reasonable will and legitimate interests must always be respected.

2279   Even if death is thought imminent, the ordinary care owed to a sick person cannot be legitimately interrupted. The use of painkillers to alleviate the sufferings of the dying, even at the risk of shortening their days, can be morally in conformity with human dignity if death is not willed as either an end or a means, but only foreseen and tolerated as inevitable. Palliative care is a special form of disinterested charity. As such it should be encouraged.

In 2001 the United States Conference of Catholic Bishops issued a revised edition of *Ethical and Religious Directives for Catholic Healthcare Services* that echoed the words of that *Catechism*.

57.   A person may forgo extraordinary or disproportionate means of preserving life. Disproportionate means are those that in the patient's judgment do not offer a reasonable hope of benefit or entail an excessive

burden, or impose excessive expense on the family or the community.

59. Euthanasia is an action or omission that of itself or by intention causes death in order to alleviate suffering. . . . Dying patients who request euthanasia should receive loving care, psychological and spiritual support, and appropriate remedies for pain and other symptoms so that they can live with dignity until the time of natural death.

A Catholic ethicist, Richard McCormick, S.J., has presented his interpretation of the term "extraordinary:"

The term "extraordinary" pertains to all medicines, treatments, and operations that cannot be obtained or used without excessive expense, pain or other inconvenience, or that if used would not offer a reasonable hope of benefit.

The Example of Pope John Paul II

Dr. Greg F. Burke, a Pennsylvania internist, cited the medical care provided to Pope John Paul II in his last months on earth as a rather marvelous example of these Catholic teachings on end-of-life issues. Writing in the November 2005 issue of *Ethics and Medics* he states:

In his final two months, he was hospitalized twice, had a tracheotomy tube inserted, and eventually was assisted in nutrition with a feeding tube. What was evident to me beyond any doubt was that his physicians, with his consent, had embarked on an aggressive course of action to deal with his respiratory compromise. I cannot be sure that all physicians would have done the same thing, given the Holy Father's multiple co-morbidities, yet the tracheotomy may have added some weeks to his life-weeks, we now know, which had a great impact on the world.

That changed, however, in the final forty-eight hours of the pope's life.

> The Pope was critically and deathly ill, but at this time he did not return to Gemelli Polyclinic for vaso-pressors (intravenous drugs to raise blood pressure), respiratory support with a ventilator or other heroic measures. The Holy Father chose to stay in his own home, (I would like to believe, with the advice of his personal physicians). The prognosis was grave, and the burden of treatment seemingly outweighed any potential short-termed prolongation of life. At that point, death was no longer to be resisted, but welcomed as the necessary transition of a Christian life into eternity.

In summary, the Holy Father concurred with the physicians' decision to use extraordinary or heroic measures to prolong his life. However, when these efforts seemed disproportionate to the outcome, less a benefit and more a burden to the Holy Father, the doctors, presumably with his approval, discontinued them.

Nutrition and Hydration

The Teri Schiavo situation drew national attention to these moral matters, but especially to the difficult question of nutrition and hydration. Prior to public statements about that specific case, however, the United States Conference of Catholic Bishops in 2001 had issued declarations, again in general fashion, about such issues including nutrition and hydration. In *Ethical and Religious Directives for Catholic Health Care Services*, the bishops write:

58. There should be a presumption in favor of providing nutrition and hydration to all patients, including patients who require medically assisted nutrition and hydration, as long as this is of sufficient benefit to outweigh the burdens involved to the patient. Pope John Paul II in 2004 also addressed the issue, remarks that were particularly of interest because of the Schiavo situation and his own deteriorating health: I should like particularly to underline how the administration of water and food, even when provided by artificial means, always represents a natural means of preserving life, not a medical act. Its use, furthermore, should be considered, in principle, ordinary and proportionate, and as such morally obligatory, insofar as and until it is seen to have attained its proper finality, which in the present case consists in providing nourishment to the patient and alleviation of his suffering.

The Holy Father's words prompted the following commentaries from a variety of sources. They demonstrate quite clearly some different interpretations with reference to the vexing questions surrounding nutrition and hydration.

a. **The Hospice Foundation**, in *Living with Grief*, made these observations:
Within the Roman Catholic tradition, the question of whether to withhold or withdraw artificial nutrition and hydration from patients in various circumstances has not been definitively answered. The U.S. Bishops' Pro-Life Committee stated in 1992, "We hold for a presumption in favor of providing medical assisted nutrition and hydration to patients who need it, which presumption would yield in cases where such procedures have no medically reasonable hope of sustaining life or pose excessive risks of burdens."

However, others within this tradition are strongly opposed to the withdrawal of tube feedings, particularly when patients are in a persistent vegetative state. Some Roman Catholic commentators consider the withdrawal of such feedings a form of intentional killing (Grisez, 1998). This question has been raised repeatedly in public, especially in connection with several legal cases in the United States. In 2004, the pope stated in a speech that did not carry the authoritative weight of an encyclical that patients in a persistent vegetative state must be provided with nutrition and hydration. (Wooden, 2004). Some take this statement to mean that tube feedings and other forms of artificial nutrition and hydration are always to be considered "ordinary" forms of care and hence required. However, others maintain that it does not mean the use of a feeding tube is obligatory in every circumstance (Thavis, 2004).

Note: It should be mentioned that the Catholic ethicist Richard McCormick, S.J., quoted earlier, differs in his viewpoint from Grisez and those of other Roman Catholic commentators cited above. He states that withdrawal of artificial nutrition and hydration to terminally ill patients is not killing but allowing to die (McCormick, 1997).

b. **Rev. Michael D. Place**, former president of the Catholic Health Association, writing in *Commonweal*, remarked: Your editorial "Extraordinary Means" (April 8) captures the careful nuances of Catholic moral reflection on end-life care. It is unfortunate that this nuance has not been present in the general discussion of the tragic case of Terri Schiavo. As your editorial notes, many people have incorrectly cited Pope John Paul II's March 2004 statement at a conference in Rome as the last word on this issue. In that statement the pope said that providing artificial nutrition and hydration for PVS patients "in principle" is to be considered morally obligatory. A better translation of the Latin phrase might be "as a general rule." However translated, it is clear that the papal statement does not eliminate the need for ethical reflection and discernment on the specifics of each case. Such discernment could well conclude that, in a particular instance, artificial nutrition and hydration is not obligatory. Similarly, as the editorial notes, papal statements must be studied . . . in the context of previous and subsequent papal statements. On November 12, 2004, the Holy Father, addressing a Vatican conference on palliative care, reaffirmed that a "decision not to start or halt treatment will be deemed ethically correct if the treatment is ineffective or obviously disproportionate to the aims of sustaining life or recovering health." While the focus of this address was not the same as the March statement, it does present the larger ethical context within which the earlier address is to be studied.

c.   **Dr. John Harvey**, Catholic theologian and medical doctor who chairs the bioethics committee at Georgetown University Hospital in Washington, commented on the words of Pope John Paul II:

I was at that conference, took part, and gave a paper there, and it's important to understand that the words of the Holy Father were interpreted in many different ways, so that it's hard to really come to the conclusion of what he exactly said to everyone. He talked very carefully and said in principle, food and water is ordinary treatment. It's not medical treatment, and therefore it's part of comfort care and must always be used—but in principle, which means there are conditions and times when it can be omitted.

—"Voices" in *Syracuse Catholic Sun*, April 28–May 4, 2005

d. **The Australian Catholic Bishops**, through two committees, one for Doctrine and Morals and the other for Health Care, issued this statement:

In summary, the Pope's statement is an application of traditional Catholic teaching, and says neither that nutrition and hydration must always be given, nor that they are never to be given, to unresponsive and/or incompetent patients. Rather, the Pope affirms the presumption in favor of giving nutrition and hydration to all patients, even by artificial means, while recognizing that in particular cases this presumption gives way to the recognition that the provision of nutrition and hydration would be futile or unduly burdensome.

I hope this chapter will prove helpful to those who wrestle with these complex but critical medical-moral issues.

three

Living Wills, Health Care Proxies, and Organ Donations

Dr. Joel Potash grew up in a small Jewish section of town, surrounded by a mostly Catholic Massachusetts community. After finishing high school, he attended and was graduated first from Dartmouth and later Boston University's School of Medicine. Through more than forty years of medicine, he has worked in a small village as a physician, practiced family medicine in a Catholic hospital, directed a medical residency program, taught in two different hospitals, served as the medical director for Hospice of Central New York and now, nearing retirement, is a member of the faculty of the Center for Bioethics and Humanities of SUNY Upstate Medical University in Syracuse. His varied medical ministry has given him enormous experience and a wonderful reputation concerning end-of-life issues.

That expertise, of course, embraces health care proxies and organ donations. He mentions that only 20 percent of Americans have health care proxies and even some of those who possess them neglect to bring the necessary, signed documents with them when they enter a hospital. Why this reluctance? Dr. Potash thinks that Americans still hesitate to face the question of their mortality and, in addition, cling to their independence. Admitting the need for some assistance leads to a sense of dependence. He likes to remind listeners that as infants and young children, we are totally dependent for a lengthy period of time. In our later and sometimes poor health years, we return to that state of dependence. Dr. Potash states that in a way it is payback time for children to take care of parents.

Dr. Potash sees the need for support or advocacy or a proxy during three stages. In the first stage, while still quite alert and in general possession of our faculties, we may need hospital care. That can be a somewhat frightening experience. In a hospital setting, we are basically strangers among a group of strangers and are cared for often by an understaffed and overworked professional workforce. Moreover, our mental, physical, and emotional status may be slightly below par. Because of these various factors, we really need someone to be an advocate, a person we can trust, who cares about us and who understands our needs.

In the second stage, our health condition may have further deteriorated. We now are more dependent and, while still alert and fairly competent, we are not quite as clear in our thinking and our ability to make choices. Once again, someone who knows us, cares about us, and is aware of our wishes should be there in an advocacy position. Dr. Potash mentions the example of a close relative of his who had a fall, surgery, and several trips to a nursing home. In each instance, his own intervention as an advocate, more than as a doctor, was needed to make sure that some things were cared for that might have been missed because of the busyness and the pressures on health care personnel.

In the third stage, we have lost use of our faculties and need someone to speak on our behalf. This is precisely when a legitimate health care proxy is needed. To identify such a proxy, we again need someone who knows us and cares about us, but who also has visited with us and other members of the family during our more coherent days. In that way, both the proxy and the family know what our wishes are and can better execute them. The proxy document simply places those desires in print and gives the designated person the legal ability to make these decisions.

The lack of an appropriate health care proxy may not be as devastating as the absence of a will, as we discussed in our first chapter. But, as became very public in the Terri Schiavo case, the absence of a clear and legitimate health care proxy and living will can result in enormous challenges and difficulties for all concerned.

Several incidents in my personal life over the past few years confirm the accuracy of Dr. Potash's description of the **first stage** involving advocacy and support. The initial one involved diagnosis and treatment of a rare bone marrow cancer called

Waldenstom's Macroglobulinemia, which is treatable, but incurable. The second incident dealt with a kidney stone, my first and so far only encounter with that very painful experience. The third occurred the day after Thanksgiving when I slipped on some ice and fractured the wrist on my left arm. Since that is my dominant hand, this raised additional problems beyond the pain, treatment, and recovery.

Dr. Potash was right on target: even in this first stage, one is alert, but still somewhat subpar physically, emotionally, and mentally. The need for a person who knows us and cares about us is critical. That individual can speak on our behalf as an advocate and also assist us when in some ways we are quite helpless. This could entail transportation, negotiating complicated paperwork, which would include completing a medical history, and assistance in other countless ways particularly during the early challenges of the event.

The **second stage** is similar to the first, but with a greater intensity. The ill person is still conscious and alert, but there has been greater deterioration of the faculties, both physically and emotionally. Those in the early to middle stages of Alzheimer's disease would be a case in point. They are still mentally alert, but their memory has slipped slightly or even significantly, and they are in greater need of an advocate and support person. A classic book by Nancy L. Mace and Peter V. Rabins called, *The Thirty-Six Hour Day: A Family Guide Caring For Persons With Alzheimer's Disease, Related Dementing Illnesses and Memory Loss in Later Life*, details both the challenges of what would be a kind of second stage as described above and some of the best ways for dealing with it.

The **third stage** involves persons who are no longer alert, whose physical conditions have greatly deteriorated, and who are unable to make rational decisions. This is precisely why we have need for health care proxies. We will examine them below in some detail.

In all three stages, nevertheless, the common burdens yield a growing sense of dependence and very often a reluctance to give up one's independence. Moreover, they highlight the need for someone or perhaps several persons who really care about us, know our desires, and can be depended upon as advocates to speak on our behalf or, when the situation develops, to decide for us.

A Living Will

The Excellus Blue Cross/Blue Shield Company, a health insurance provider in upstate New York, working collaboratively with a Rochester health care forum, produced a booklet titled *Advanced Care Planning: Compassion and Support at the End-of-Life*. It includes a sample "New York Health Care Proxy" and a "New York Living Will." Laws about these matters vary from state to state. In New York, for example, a health care proxy has legal force, but the living will only moral suasion.

Here is a sample living will document, adapted from that booklet mentioned above. It contains the descriptions and desires of the person completing such a document.

Sample Living Will

I, (your name)_____, being of sound mind, make this statement as a directive to be followed if I become permanently unable to participate in decisions regarding my own medical care. These instructions reflect my firm and settled commitment to decline medical treatment under the circumstances indicated below:

I direct my attending physician to withhold or withdraw treatment that merely prolongs my dying, if I should be in an incurable or **irreversible mental or physical condition with no reasonable expectation of recovery,** including but not limited to: **(a) a terminal condition; (b) a permanently unconscious condition; or (c) a minimally conscious condition in which I am permanently unable to make decisions or express my wishes.**

I direct that my treatment be limited to measures to keep me comfortable and to relieve pain, including any pain that might occur by withholding or withdrawing treatment.

While I understand that I am not legally required to be specific about future treatments, if I am in the condition(s) described above I feel especially strong about the following forms of treatment:

(Cross out any statements that do not reflect your wishes)

I do not want cardiac resuscitation.

I do not want mechanical respiration.

I do not want artificial nutrition and hydration.

I do not want antibiotics.

However, I **do want** maximum pain relief, even if it may hasten my death.

Other instructions: *(Add here any additional directives you want followed.)*

These directions express my legal right to refuse treatment, under the laws of this state. I intend my instructions to be carried out, unless I have rescinded them in a new writing or by clearly indicating that I have changed my mind.

(Sign and date the document and print your address.)

Signed _____

Date _____

Address _____

Witnessing Procedure

I declare that the person who signed this document appeared to execute this living will willingly and free from duress. He or she signed (or asked another to sign for him or her) this document in my presence.

(Witnesses must sign and date this document and print their addresses.)

Witness 1 _____

Address _____

Witness 2 _____

Address _____

A Health Care Proxy

The statement for assigning a health care proxy describes the situation of a person who would be in what we have categorized the third stage. That individual needs a proxy, agent, or support person. A duly signed and witnessed document would also be extremely beneficial, even essential, as has been exemplified in the case of Terri Schiavo.

The person making the proxy should gather together both the agent and the substitute or fill-in agent together with as many members of the family as possible for a discussion about this proxy and/or living will. In that way a number of persons will know the intentions and desires of the one filling out the document or documents. When and if that proxy is implemented, it will make it easier for the proxy or fill-in agent to make decisions knowing that a good number of family members concur with the desires of the person who has assigned the proxy.

As noted above, it is critical that the actual signed and witnessed proxy statement accompany the patient to the hospital or health care facility for communication to medical personnel. The person designated in the proxy should not only know and care about the ill individual, but also be assertive and even aggressive in carrying out those wishes. Sometimes health care professionals may question that person's interference with medical procedures. Having the document in hand should help alleviate this difficulty.

Sample Health Care Proxy

I,_____ , hereby appoint:

(Your name here)

_____

(Name, home address and telephone number of agent)

as my health care agent to make any and all health care decisions for me, except to the extent that I state otherwise. **My agent does know my wishes regarding artificial nutrition and hydration.**

This health care proxy shall take effect in the event I become unable to make my own health care decisions.

(Add personal instructions below, if there are any.)

(2) Optional instructions: I direct my agent to make health care decisions in accord with my wishes and limitations as stated below, or as he or she otherwise knows.

Alternate Agent

(3) Name of substitute or fill-in agent if the person I appoint above is unable, unwilling or unavailable to act as my health care agent.

Name, home address, and telephone number of alternate agent

Organ Donation (optional)

(4) Donation of organs at death

Upon my death:

[ ] I **do not** wish to donate my organs, tissues or parts.

[ ] I **do** wish to be an organ donor and upon my death I wish to donate:

[ ] (a) Any needed organs, tissues, or parts; **OR**

[ ] (b) The following organs, tissues, or parts

_____

_____

[ ] (c) My gift is for the following purposes:

*Put a line through any of the following you **do not** want.*

Transplant

Therapy

Research

Education

Duration or condition(s)

(5) Unless I revoke it, this proxy shall remain in effect indefinitely, or until the date or condition I have stated below. This proxy shall expire on:

_____

_____

_____

Give specific date or conditions, if desired.
Signature *Sign and date your document and print your address*

Date _____

Address _____

Witnessing Procedure (Must be eighteen or older)

I declare that the person who signed this document appeared to execute the proxy willingly and free from duress. He or she signed (or asked another to sign for him or her) this document in my presence. I am not the person appointed as proxy by this document.

(Witnesses must sign and date this document and print their addresses.)

Witness 1 _____

Address _____

Witness 2 _____

Address _____

Organ Donations

The *Catechism of the Catholic Church* addresses the question of organ donation:

2296 Organ donation after death is a noble and meritorious act and is to be encouraged as an expression of generous solidarity. It is not morally acceptable if the donor or the proxy has not given explicit consent. Moreover, it is not morally admissible directly to bring about the disabling mutilation or a death of a human being even in order to delay the death of other persons.

The sample health care proxy form presented above specifically details donation of organs or of the body itself as an option. This donation of the body, called "An anatomical gift to a medical center for use in preparing future physicians or health care personnel," has a certain uniqueness to it. The

Upstate Medical University in Syracuse provides a booklet with an explanation and some details about this specific donation of one's body. It includes the following directives:

- That medical university will not accept the donation of someone who is under twenty-one years of age, is excessively obese, has an active communicable disease, is infected with or is a carrier of contagious diseases such as Hepatitis B or C, Tuberculosis, or HIV. Nor will it accept the body if the number of donations exceeds the capacity of its facility to effectively and safely handle additional donations.

- A donation can be accepted only if the next of kin or another responsible party is willing to abide by the donor's wishes and release the body to the medical center. Under New York state law, the next of kin is obligated to abide by the donor's wishes and donate the body.

- Bodies donated to Upstate's Anatomical Gift Program will be used primarily for the teaching of anatomy. Health professionals ranging from first year medical and physical therapy students to residents and faculty at the Upstate Medical University benefit greatly from the opportunity to engage in active, hands-on learning about the intricacies of the human body.

- Upon the donor's death, the next of kin or another person responsible for arrangements, should request that the hospital or a doctor contact a licensed funeral director to make arrangements for transporting the body to the university building within forty-eight hours. A licensed funeral director will also need to deliver the release of remains permission form, a return of cremains form, a photocopy of the death certificate (signed by the attending physician), and a burial permit.

- Only a licensed funeral director may transport a body. As noted, the funeral director is responsible to obtain the necessary documents. These forms must accompany a donated body.

- No casket or other container needs to be purchased in order to have the body transported to the University.

- Upon completion of the studies on that body, the remains will be cremated at the expense of the medical center. If requested, the cremains of the donor will then be returned to the family or to the funeral director for burial.

- The time frame for the cremains to be returned will vary, with a maximum of two years.

Sample Anatomical Gift Pledge Form

This statement is to certify that I wish my body, at the time of my death, to be transported and delivered to the (*name of institution appears here*) to be used as an unrestricted gift for (*intended purpose of the donation is named here, for example, the advancement of medical education and research*). If I am geographically closer to another (*type of institution such as medical college*) at the time of death, I am (I am not) willing to have my body delivered there.

In connection with this pledge, I have received and reviewed the Anatomical Gift Program brochure, I authorize my physician, or hospital, to release my lab reports and patient history relating to illness at time of death should this information be necessary to rule out communicable disease.

Donor name (please print):

_____

❏ Mr. ❏ Mrs. ❏ Ms. ❏ Miss_____

Donor signature: _____

Date of pledge:_____

Witness signature: _____

Witness signature: _____

Social Security
number of donor: _____

Date of birth of donor: _____

Present address of donor: _____

_____

Phone number(s) of donor: _____

___ Yes, I have discussed my wishes with my family, and they agree with my decision.

Elan Salzhauer, a former SUNY Upstate Medical University student, wrote this touching tribute to those who have made donations of their body to the University:

> You have given four individuals the answers to their dreams. With each day . . . we come closer to understanding the process by which we live and die. Your gift is the key to our education. You are our most important class—your silence is our most important lecture—you are our most interesting professor. You are a valiant person and I will never, ever forget you. For the body you have donated so that I may one day help others, I thank you from the depths of my soul. May God bless you for the ultimate and priceless gift.

four

Cremation

During their courtship more than three decades ago, Ann and Sam Buranich talked often about a dream or vision they shared. She, an elementary public school teacher, and he, a graduate of both business college and mortuary institute, hoped to establish a funeral home in their neighborhood. Experienced advisors warned them that it would take a generation to do so. That prediction proved absolutely accurate.

Soon after their marriage, with the help of funds from some relatives, they were able to obtain a zone change, purchase a building, and renovate it for their purposes. They lived in an apartment above the new funeral home and, although both were necessarily employed elsewhere, began to operate their business on a full-time basis right from the start. Eventually Ann left her teaching position and became a full-time stay-at-home mom for their two children. Sam continued his position as a middle manager in a large company located near the funeral home.

The clients were few in the beginning, although there was a gradual increase. With Ann's assistance, Sam was able to take care of these few calls during lunch hours and after work. However, when the numbers reached approximately thirty calls annually, it became too taxing to carry on the funeral operation while Sam was still working for the other company. They then took a deep step in faith: he resigned from his position and became full-time director of the funeral home.

There were many lean years as they tried to pay off the mortgage, raise the family, and obtain a house for themselves separate from the funeral home. Ann once said, "As long as we can have bread and butter on the table, it is worthwhile pursuing our vision." Now, after more than three decades of following their dream, they service more than one hundred families each year and have a number of employees to assist them. Their clientele are mostly Roman Catholic neighborhood people. However, only in the past dozen years have there been increased requests for cremation. Prior to this, most people judged that the Church opposed such a procedure and never sought that option.

Today, about 20 percent of the funerals at Buranich's involve cremation. They have worked out a system that allows for the preferred option of having the body at church for a funeral Mass and at the same time saves families the significant cost of purchasing a casket. A rental casket that has a replaceable interior is made available to families. With this the Buranichs are able to make the body available for the viewing or calling hours, transfer it to the church for the service, and afterwards take the casket back to the funeral home. There the interior box with the body is removed and transported to the crematory. They also assist families in developing a reverent way of burying the cremains.

In this way the Buranichs are able to offer a funeral service that is in accord with the liturgical traditions and regulations of the Catholic Church and at the same time responds to the wishes of the family for cremation.

Church Prohibition and Approval

The Buranich Funeral Home experienced a significant growth in cremations in just three decades. This mirrors the shift toward cremation as a choice in burials throughout the United States. About one quarter of Americans select cremation, and it is projected that by 2010, the number will rise to a third of all funerals.

For many years, the Catholic Church prohibited cremation mostly because there was a concern that those choosing that option were prompted by a denial of the resurrection. Moreover, the practice in itself tended to undercut the Church's preference for the presence of the body at the celebration of all the funeral rites as well as its preference for burial in the ground. The Church prefers ground burial for several reasons. Here are perhaps the most compelling. First, we have the example of

Jesus, who was laid in the tomb. Second, there is the fact that these bodies were once washed in baptism, anointed with the oil of salvation, and fed with the Bread of Life. They deserve to be carefully prepared for dignified burial. Third, we have the long-held teaching that the body is a temple of the Holy Spirit and is destined for future glory at the resurrection of the dead. And fourth, a conviction that the presence of the body during calling hours and at all the funeral rites helps mourners face the reality of a person's death.

Since the prohibition of cremation was clearly understood and widely observed for years by Catholics (laity and clergy alike), there were understandably no official rituals for the few funeral services in which cremation was chosen once the prohibition was lifted. The rather rapid increase in cremations after that point created challenges for those in parish ministry. Many, perhaps most, Catholic clergy made pastoral adaptations in response to a family's request for a funeral service connected with cremation. Those who did so, however, were conscious of a tension between the church's official position regarding burial, the understandable liturgical void, and the actual situation facing them.

Fortunately, those conflicts were resolved in 1997. The American Bishops requested from Rome an indult or permission to allow the cremated remains of a body at funeral liturgies in the United States. They also prepared an Appendix to the *Order of Christian Funerals* for use with cremation. The indult was granted and the Appendix approved. The U.S. bishops then implemented the permission and published the new rite in the same year.

The *Order of Christian Funerals with Cremation Rite* (OCF) provides clear and detailed guidance for a funeral service when cremation has been chosen. Here are some of the specific details addressed there,

- *Permitted, Not Preferred*

Numbers #413–415 of the *Cremation Rite* summarize the Church's position and attitude:

> Although the Church now permits cremation, it does not enjoy the same value as burial of the body. The Church clearly prefers and urges that the body of the deceased be present for the funeral rites, since the presence of the human body better expresses the values that the Church affirms in those rites.
>
> The Church's teaching in regard to the human body as well as the Church's preference for burial of the body should be a regular part of catechesis on all levels and pastors should make particular efforts to preserve this important teaching.
>
> Sometimes, however, it is not possible for the body to be present for the Funeral Mass. When extraordinary circumstances make the cremation of a body the only feasible choice, pastoral sensitivity must be exercised by priests, deacons, and others who minister to the family of the deceased.

- *Various Options*

The Church prefers that cremation take place after the funeral liturgy, but recognizes that circumstances sometimes dictate cremation preceding the funeral liturgy. It provides ritual directions and texts for both situations (*OCF* #418–431).

- *Reverence for the Cremains*

Article #417 treats in detail the respect or reverence with which the cremated remains should be treated:

> The cremated remains of a body should be treated with the same respect given to the human body from which they come. This includes the use of a worthy vessel to contain the ashes, the manner in which they are carried, the care and attention to appropriate placement and transport, and the final disposition. The cremated remains should be buried in a grave or entombed in a mausoleum or columbarium. The practice of scattering cremated remains on the sea, from the air, or on the ground, or keeping cremated remains in the home of a relative or friend of the deceased are not the reverent disposition the Church requires. Whenever possible, appropriate means for recording with dignity the memory of the deceased should be adopted, such as a plaque or stone which records the name of the deceased.

Donation of the Body: A Unique Challenge

Those who "in a noble and meritorious act" (CCC #2296) choose to donate their entire bodies to science or to a medical school for use by students studying to become physicians understand that the body is taken immediately upon death to the recipient institution. There it is stored for future use. After one or two years, the school cremates the remains and will either bury the ashes in a local cemetery or return them to the next of kin. This process would seem to suggest two services—a funeral Mass or service at the time of death with no body or ashes present and a memorial Mass or service with the ashes a year or two later.

five

Postponing Eternity

Kevin Murphy grew up in a small city of upstate New York, a place best known for its production of Nestle Chocolates, Miller Beer, and Sealright containers. He entered the seminary immediately after high school and was ordained in his middle twenties. Devout, serious, and somewhat traditional, he displayed a very sensitive concern for the sick and homebound in parish life.

Father Murphy believed that the rite for the Anointing of the Sick was greatly underused. When celebrating the ritual himself, he encouraged all present to place their hands one after the other upon the head of the seriously ill person following his own silent imposition of hands. Sadly, he was diagnosed with a severe and painful cancer after only three decades of life. Father Murphy spent his last year as a hospital patient. Even there, however, he continued his healing ministry, frequently walking down a corridor with an IV pole in one hand and a ritual book plus the holy oil for anointing in the other. He died, quite symbolically, at thirty-three.

The Power of Healing Prayer

As a young priest I believed in miracles, including those that brought about a restoration of health. However, I thought that this happened only in sacred shrines like Lourdes in France or the Oratory in Montreal and through the intercession of holy people like Mary, the Mother of God, or the Canadian, Brother Andre Bessette. That changed for me in the 1960s, a decade after I had been ordained as a parish priest.

Father Francis McNutt, a well-known preacher and writer, outlined in his book *Healing* a biblical case for the power of healing prayer. His logic was unassailable, convinced me, and caused a shift in my own way of praying for those in any kind of trouble. His simple but potent argument could be summarized in this way:

- Jesus often touched the sick, healed people, and cured many of all kinds of diseases (Lk 7:20–33).

- Christ gave that power to the twelve apostles (Lk 9:1–2).

- The Lord then extended this ability to the seventy-two (Lk 10:1, 8–9).

- God tells us that all those who believe and lay hands upon the sick will cure them (Mk 16:17–18).

Relatively soon after reading McNutt's book, I had an experience that will help to illustrate the transformation in my own approach to those ill or troubled persons who ask for prayer. During the intermission of a symphony concert, a parishioner approached me in the vestibule. The woman said that she had breast cancer, was scheduled for surgery on Monday, and, being deeply anxious, had not slept for two weeks. Would I pray for her? Of course.

I then placed one hand upon her arm and the other on the arm of her husband and spoke a simple, spontaneous prayer for their inner peace and courage as well as for her physical healing. It was neither long nor dramatic. I telephoned her home on that Monday night. To my surprise, she answered. When they were preparing her for surgery, the lump had apparently disappeared. Was it a fluke? A false diagnosis? A miraculous healing? Who knows, except God.

Before McNutt's book, I would have assured her of a remembrance in my prayers with the intention of recalling this woman in my mind at Mass. Now I always pray on the spot, in a softly vocal way, usually touching the person or persons as I utter the words. While such a prayerful encounter does not always produce the remarkable results that this woman experienced, I usually witness tears flowing from the ill or troubled persons. It obviously connects with them on the deepest level of their being.

Anointing of the Sick

During the Church's first millennium, the ritual for anointing the sick was intended to restore ill persons to health so they could rejoin the active community and participate at Mass. That approach shifted in the Middle Ages when it became the ritual preparing a person for eternity—the last rites, as it were—the sacrament to be received at death's door. As recently as the 1950s, people frequently resisted requesting this sacrament precisely because in their common understanding it meant that death was imminent. When either or both the dying person or family members were in denial of the patient's terminal condition, they understandably hesitated to call the priest.

In 1964 the Church returned partially to its earlier approach when bishops at the Second Vatican Council decreed that this rite may "more properly be called 'anointing of the sick'" and "is not a sacrament for those who are at the point of death." In Chapter 7, we will deal specifically with the Church's official last rites.

In 1972 the Vatican published the Latin texts of new rites for the anointing and care of the sick. These texts, compiled in *Pastoral Care of the Sick and Viaticum* (PCS), were translated into English and adapted for use the United States in 1983. The numbers after the different sections below indicate the pertinent article in the General Instruction of that ritual.

- *What are the effects of the Anointing of the Sick?*

This sacrament gives the grace of the Holy Spirit to sick persons. Through that grace they are helped and saved, sustained by trust in God, strengthened against temptation of the Evil One, and relieved of their anxiety over death. Moreover, they are able to bear suffering bravely and also to fight against it. In addition, they may receive a return to physical health. Finally, this sacrament likewise forgives sins and completes Christian penance (*PCS* #6).

- *Who receives this sacrament?*

Those who are seriously ill because of sickness or old age should receive the sacrament. Children who have reached the age of reason (the same criterion for First Communion) may likewise be recipients of this anointing. The term "seriously ill" should be interpreted in liberal, relaxed fashion; it includes, for example, people anticipating major surgery. A footnote in the ritual summarizes the proper approach. "The sacrament may and should be given to anyone whose health is seriously impaired; on the other hand, it may not be given indiscriminately or to any person whose health is not seriously impaired" (*PCS* #8–14).

- *How is the sacrament celebrated?*

A priest is the only proper minister of this sacrament (*PCS* #16). There are three fundamental elements involved.

1. Prayer of faith

An introduction, biblical readings, and various prayers are meant to stir up the participants' faith in the presence of the Risen, Healing Christ in this sacrament. The community asks for God's help for the sick in a spirit of trust.

> The entire Church is made present in this community—represented by at least the priest, family, friends, and others—assembled to pray for those to be anointed. If they are able, the sick persons should also join in this prayer (*PCS,* #106).

2. Laying on of hands

Jesus frequently healed the sick by a word, a touch, or by laying his hands upon the sick person. In this sacrament, just prior to the actual anointing with oil, the priest silently lays hands upon the ill individual. In the opening story of this chapter, we noted the example of Father Kevin Murphy. Although a priest of upstate New York, he has inspired many clergy across the country, including this writer, to follow his practice of inviting those present for the anointing also to lay their hands upon the sick person. After the priest has done so in silence, friends, family members, and loved ones are invited to likewise lay their hands upon the sick individual, also in silence.

3. Anointing with oil of the sick

When possible, the priest anoints the forehead and hands of the ill individual. In certain circumstances another suitable part of the body may be anointed (PCS, #5). As the priest anoints, he speaks the prescribed words for this sacrament:

> Through this holy anointing
> may the Lord in his love and mercy help you
> with the grace of the Holy Spirit.
>
> May the Lord who frees you from sin
> Save you and raise you up (*PCS*, #25).

The bishop at the cathedral church ordinarily blesses the oil of the sick during Holy Week. Each parish church and every priest subsequently obtains a portion of that oil for use in this sacrament. Consequently there is a symbolic link between the priest, the local bishop, other bishops throughout the world, and ultimately the Holy

Father. Thus the whole church is, as it were, part of this praying, anointing rite. A prayer to conclude the anointing rite nicely summarizes the healing and comforting thrust of the sacrament:

> Father in heaven,
> through this holy anointing
> grant N. comfort in his/her suffering.
> When he/she is afraid, give him/her courage,
> when afflicted, give him/her patience,
> when dejected, afford him/her hope.
> and when alone, assure him/her
> of the support of your holy people.
> We ask this through Christ our Lord (*PCS*, #125)

six
——

Heart Light as a Feather: Forgiveness and Reconciliation

I hope this letter finds you in good health and spirits. I am one of the many people whose spirit you touched this past week at our parish mission. No "Hallmark greeting card" could express my great appreciation and gratitude toward you. To say my soul and inner feelings are "as light as a feather" would be an understatement. The only feeling I can compare my reconciliation experience to is what I felt at these two important times in my life:

1. The day I was married eighteen years ago to my high school sweetheart.

2. The birth of our beautiful daughter, who is now sixteen years old.

For some unexplained reason in my teenage years, I came to the conclusion that any time I needed forgiveness, all I had to do was pray directly to God and ask for his forgiveness. I can honestly say that I will still do this, but will also receive the sacrament of Penance at least on a seasonal basis. I am a firm believer that priests have a gift to be a strong connection directly to our Lord Jesus Christ that allows the feeling of complete forgiveness, one that cannot be felt by praying alone.

Thanks again for changing my life at the young age of forty. You and this mission will be a lasting memory for the rest of my life.

Sin and Guilt

Some years ago, the famous psychiatrist Karl Menninger questioned and bemoaned the disappearance of the word sin from the vocabulary and attitude of Americans. He echoed a much earlier papal commentary made in the middle of the last century by Pope Pius XII. Pius declared then that the loss of a sense of sin was one of contemporary society's greatest failures or erroneous trends. The fact is that a healthy, but not a neurotic, awareness of sin is essential for a sound Christian spirituality. Without a sense of sin there would be no conscious need to receive a sacrament that forgives sins, or a Church that preaches the infinite mercy of God, or, even more radically, to embrace Jesus, the Savior, who came to free us from sin.

Because of human weakness, it is, practically speaking, impossible to avoid sin or keep the biblical commandments perfectly in our lives. We are doomed for failure in this regard. That may sound bizarre or pessimistic, but while the Ten Commandments may seem doable enough, consider these scriptural challenges:

Does anyone love God and neighbor with a whole heart?

Or totally forgive others?

Or always, immediately, and cheerfully respond to people in need?

Failure to follow these divine imperatives is a sin, if done so knowingly and willingly. To put the experience in simpler terms, sin occurs when God tells us in our hearts to do something and, with full knowledge and consent, we don't do it. Sin also occurs when God speaks to us within not to do something and, again, with complete knowledge and consent, we do it.

Guilt, a painful, penetrating, and perduring reality, follows sin. It stays with us night and day. It can rob us of peace, cause an upset stomach, or spoil a beautiful event. A contemporary therapist maintains that unacknowledged and unexpiated guilt is the ultimate source of all interior anguish. We can ignore, deny, or suppress guilt, but ultimately it will surface.

We can place guilt in two categories: Real, true, or rational guilt and unreal, false, or irrational guilt. True guilt, caused by our own real sin, requires a forgiveness that only God can give. But false guilt, of which there are many kinds, requires not so much forgiveness (perhaps none at all) as healing and even, at times, professional therapy. Some examples of this false

51

guilt are making nothing into something, raising moral mole hills into mortal sin mountains, and not letting go of sins that God forgave long ago. Taking responsibility for situations that are not our responsibility is another and common form of such irrational guilt—for instance, parents blaming themselves for their children's serious misdeeds, grown-up offspring torn by the unreasonable demands of their aging and infirm parents, or family members and friends torturing themselves with self-accusations of neglect after a loved one's suicide.

There is a commonly repeated expression or truth in our everyday lives, "no pain, no gain." Without a painful knee surgery and recuperation, we could not have the ultimate gain of painless walking; without the various self-denials required in years of study and preparation, we would never gain the title of physician; without taking the necessarily painful steps for coping with an addiction, we will not taste the gain of freedom, of being able to manage our lives. So, too, unless we taste the pain of sin and guilt, it is unlikely that we will fully appreciate the joy of God's forgiveness and freedom.

Forgiveness and Freedom

Jesus Christ came into this world not to condemn us, but to save us and set us free, to forgive our sins and heal our guilt. Hospital chaplains and parish priests often bring this hope-filled message to seriously ill patients. Quite frequently they encounter people who have been carrying a heavy burden of sin and guilt for years, but who, nevertheless, for various reasons, have never been able to bring this darkness fully to the light of God's forgiveness. In such situations, the priest, after a relatively brief exchange with the ailing patient, may then speak these words of reconciliation:

> Through the ministry of the Church, may God give
> you pardon and peace, and I absolve you from your

sins in the name of the Father, and of the Son, and of the Holy Spirit.

—Pastoral Care of the Sick, #305

The joy, relief, and freedom such absolved, forgiven, and healed individuals experience through this simple celebration of the sacrament of reconciliation is often quite transparent. They can now face their future with a profound peace and deep serenity.

Those who minister to others in this fashion are simply communicating the divine compassion that Jesus proclaimed by his actions and through his words.

Christ, on several occasions, forgave others: the criminal on the cross, promising immediate entrance into paradise, of Luke 23:39–43; the woman caught in adultery of John 8:1–11; the "sinful woman" of Luke 7:36–50; and the paralytic of Luke 5:17–26.

Jesus also frequently spoke about God's mercy. In the fifteenth chapter of Luke's gospel, Christ describes the lost sheep, coin, and son. The message at the end is identical: there is joy in heaven over one who repents. In John's gospel, the Lord says, "God did not send his Son into the world to condemn the world, but that the world might be saved through him" (Jn 3:17). These actions and teachings should not surprise us. In Matthew's gospel, an angel of the Lord told Joseph about this Son just conceived miraculously by the Holy Spirit in Mary's womb. "You are to name him Jesus, because he will save his people from their sins" (Mt 1:21). In word and deed, Christ clearly fulfilled that prediction.

Facing death and going before God to show the Lord our lives—with all our successes and failures, our ugly sins and good deeds—is a sobering event to say the least. However, to know that we have been forgiven and to believe that we will stand before our Creator, who is kind and merciful, enables us to face that future with a peaceful heart.

seven

Last Rites

John worked his entire adult life as a house painter. That occupation put food on the family table, but eventually caused serious deterioration in his respiratory system. In his last years, it became difficult for him to breathe and even to speak. Married to a Catholic and raised in a Protestant family, he had some knowledge of the Bible and a basic belief in God. However, for whatever reason, John was never baptized. His daughter called one day and requested that I visit her father, who was now bed-ridden at home and terminally ill. John had expressed to her his desire for baptism.

Shortly thereafter I knelt beside the man's low-slung bed and visited with him about his wish for this sacrament. In that brief exchange, a struggle for him because of his labored breathing, it was clear he possessed sufficient knowledge, faith, and willingness to receive baptism. Because of his critical condition, I did so then and there.

John soon entered the hospital for the last months of his life. I visited him early one evening and asked, "John, would you like me to pray with you?" He nodded affirmatively.

"Do you have a special prayer you like?" "Yes," he replied, "the green pastures prayer." In response to his request, I recited Psalm 23, the familiar Good Shepherd text.

"John I have a few other prayers. Is it all right if I say these for you?" He again nodded his head. I then bent over next to his ear and recited a few short biblical verses contained in the Church's ritual for the Commendation of the Dying, softly repeating each one several times.

"We have an everlasting home in heaven" (2 Cor 5:1).

"We shall be with the Lord forever" (1 Thes 4:17).

"We shall see God as he really is" (1 Jn 3:2).

After this last phrase, John, in a barely audible voice, whispered something. I moved close to his mouth and listened as he repeated, "How wonderful it will be to stand in the presence of God and see God as God really is." I drove home from the hospital that night deeply touched by this soul-to-soul exchange with a dying man.

Pastoral Care of the Sick

Parishioners at the San Antonio Roman Catholic Church, a parish of 2,000 families in Port Charlotte, Florida, take excellent care of their ill members. Under the leadership of their pastor and the director of pastoral care, over one hundred volunteer "Pastoral Ministers of the Holy Eucharist" bring communion on a weekly basis to those who are housebound. Those being visited may reside at their own homes or in a variety of health care institutions. The system is extremely well organized and efficient.

Every Friday, two alternating teams of these volunteers fan out around the parish and bring the consecrated host to the homebound. Because of the team approach, those being visited experience a variety of visitors, but without being overwhelmed by a constantly changing group of pastoral ministers. In addition, if members of one team are away, the other team can maintain that weekly continuity of visitation.

Each week the parish priests join one of the teams and during the course of a visit, celebrate the sacrament of the anointing of the sick. In this fashion, over the course of three months, every housebound person receives that sacrament, even more often whenever there is a negative change or serious worsening of the individual's condition. In addition, there is a monthly healing Mass for those who are able to make it to the church.

The pastoral care director maintains careful records of those who have been anointed and when they received this sacrament. That information is particularly helpful when a family member or health care person calls the parish requesting last rites for a dying person.

Last Rites

As we have seen, the Anointing of the Sick is for those who are seriously ill, not those necessarily near death. However, in the past, and unfortunately even in the present, many persons think or speak of this sacrament as the last rites. That terminology certainly makes some sick individuals or family members reluctant to summon the priest for anointing. Moreover, it is theologically inaccurate. The Church's last rites are the celebration of viaticum, the reception of the Eucharist within a special format.

The ritual book, Pastoral Care of the Sick, includes a separate chapter, "Celebration of Viaticum." Its introduction explicitly clarifies the distinction between the anointing of the sick and viaticum as the appropriate last rites of the Church:

> The celebration of the Eucharist as viaticum, food for the passage through death to eternal life, is the sacrament proper to the dying Christian. It is the completion and crown of the Christian life on this earth, signifying that the Christian follows the Lord to eternal glory and the banquet of the heavenly kingdom.

> The sacrament of the anointing of the sick should be celebrated at the beginning of a serious illness. Viaticum, celebrated when death is close, will then be better understood as the last sacrament of Christian life (PCS, # 175).

In addition to the customary prayers, biblical readings and blessings for Communion to the Sick, the Rite for Viaticum includes a remembrance of baptismal promises and the insertion of special words at the reception of communion. Viaticum means, literally, "with you on the way." The ritual describes that sacramental purpose and the words added at the time of the reception of viaticum.

> As an indication that the reception of the Eucharist by the dying Christian is a pledge of resurrection and food for the passage through death, the special words proper to viaticum are added: 'May the Lord Jesus Christ protect you and lead you to eternal life' (PCS, #181).

When someone contacts the parish priest at the church in San Antonio and requests spiritual assistance for a dying person, even calling for the last rites, the exchange and response most likely would follow this sequence:
"Is the dying person conscious or alert?"

- If the answer is yes, the priest would bring viaticum to the individual, checking first to see if the person has already been anointed.

- If the person has not been anointed, or if a significant time has elapsed since the previous anointing, or if this is a relatively sudden and different worsening of the individual's condition, the priest would also celebrate the Anointing of the Sick.

- If the person is not conscious or alert, the priest would ask if family members or friends are present. If so, even though a check of records indicate that the individual has been anointed, he would go to the location and pray with those people by the bedside of the dying person.

- If the person is not conscious or alert, has, according to their church records, been anointed, and no family or friends are present, the priest would inform the health care individual calling that there is nothing further he can do and might not travel to the spot, if other responsibilities are pressing.

- If there are latter inquiries about the spiritual care that had been given to the dying person, the priest can reply with accuracy and total honesty that the individual was surrounded by all of the Church's rites for the sick and the dying.

Prayers for the Dying

Years ago a physician advised a single woman caring for her terminally ill father, "When the time comes for your dad to die, pick him up and hold him, so that he is not alone when he finally leaves here for eternity." This certainly is the ideal—that no one is alone when the end-of-life, the moment of death, arrives. Unfortunately, that is often not the case. Family members and close friends instinctively recognize that ideal and try to be present during those final hours. However, there usually is great apprehension among them. They wonder to themselves or to each other, "What do we do? What do we say?" The Church offers some helpful suggestions for those situations:

- *Frequently touch the dying patients.*

They are drifting away, isolated, cut off from the world around them. Holding their hands, moistening their lips, and caressing their foreheads are quite natural and comforting gestures. The occasional laying of hands can recall that powerful action during the anointing of the sick that we described earlier. Gently making the Sign of the Cross often on the forehead is a reminder of a similar gesture made at baptism, that foundational sacrament that opens the gates of heaven for us.

- *Reciting short biblical phrases into their ears.*

We saw that practice illustrated in the introductory story of this chapter. The *Pastoral Care of the Sick* ritual contains nearly twenty of these phrases, brief biblical texts that have been reprinted for popular use in a small booklet, *A Thoughtful Word, A Healing Touch*. That publication describes their use in this fashion:

> The final struggle in our journey of life is a test of faith. Is there a life to come? Will I see God? How can I possibly cross the chasm between my finite human weakness and limitations and the infinite, divine majesty or holiness of God?
>
> In addition, there is an enormous need for strength to bear intense physical pain, to overcome the deep discouragement caused by a lengthy illness, or to endure the sadness of leaving behind those we love.
>
> When people are very seriously ill or near death, brief biblical texts can be of great support for them. These phrases are best recited in a slow, quiet voice, alternated with periods of silence. Since the sense of hearing often remains operative after the other faculties seem to have lost their power, the words might be spoken into the dying person's ear, with each phrase repeated two or three times before moving on to the next one.

What a great comfort to hear, for example, these words as one prepares for the leap into eternity:

> "Truly I say to you: today you will be with me in paradise," says the Lord Jesus (Lk 23:43).

eight

A Comforting Farewell

A man in his fifties had recently suffered a heart attack. When the local parish offered an evening session on caring for the seriously ill and preparing the funeral liturgy, he and his wife decided to attend. About a year later he and his family were at their summer lakeside home. In the late afternoon, his ten-year-old daughter with her cousin asked to go out in the rowboat for a short while. The father agreed, but cautioned them not to go too far from the shore. He remained there watching the two girls. A speedboat pulling a water skier rapidly approached the area and passed the two youngsters. The skier fell and the boat turned to pick him up. Tragically, the driver didn't notice the small rowboat, crashed into it, and instantly killed both children.

The next day, a very sensitive funeral director and the parish priest sat around a table with the stunned and stricken family discussing burial arrangements. After a half hour of working out some details, the wife, remembering that earlier session and still having a booklet for preparing the funeral Mass, suggested that the priest, also a family friend, read one of the biblical passages from it. When he hesitated because of tears streaming down his own face, the father picked up the booklet, glanced through the scripture readings and read an excerpt from 1 Thessalonians (4:13–18) about hope, faith, and resurrection. The grief-stricken man concluded with these final words of that section, "Therefore, console one another with these words." They later decided to use this passage as one of the biblical texts for the funeral Mass and also had it printed on the back of their daughter's memorial card.

San Antonio Parish in Port Charlotte, Florida, not only takes impressive care of its homebound parishioners, it also encourages members to pre-plan their funeral arrangements. Since many are elderly and are transplants from other areas of the country, their children and relatives often live at great distances from them. Having decisions about the church service and burial done in advance greatly alleviates the stress and difficulties for survivors when death finally comes. The parish has a form to facilitate the process. It keeps the complete document on file and recommends that copies be sent to the closest relatives and to the funeral director(s) of choice. Sometimes two funeral directors are involved if burial will be in a place at some distance from where the funeral takes place.

Encouraged Participation

Prior to the Second Vatican Council, the parish church provided funeral services, with the rite frequently called a Requiem Mass. However, the surviving family members had only minimal input into the liturgical celebration. Most often, the texts and ceremonies were standard and nearly identical for each funeral. That changed radically with the publication of the Order of Christian Funerals in the early 1970s.

This revised set of rites provided a rich variety of prayers, readings, and blessings from which to choose. It also explicitly urged, in its introduction, that family members of the deceased be actively involved with planning and participating in the funeral liturgy.

> Whenever possible, ministers should involve the family in planning the funeral rites: in the choice of texts and rites provided in the ritual, in the selection of music for the rites, and in the designation of liturgical ministers.

> Planning of the funeral rites may take place during the visit of the pastor or other minister at some appropriate time after the death and before the vigil service. Ministers should explain to the family the meaning and significance of each of the funeral rites,

especially the vigil, the funeral liturgy, and the rite of committal.

If pastoral and personal consideration allow, the period before death may be an appropriate time to plan the funeral rites with the family and even with the family member who is dying. Although planning the funeral before death should be approached with sensitivity and care, it can have the effect of helping the one who is dying and the family face the reality of death with Christian hope. It can also help relieve the family of numerous details after the death and may allow them to benefit more fully from the celebration of the funeral rites (OCF, #17).

An Essential First Step

During the past forty years as a pastor in three different parishes—a small-city faith community, a large suburban church, and a center-city Cathedral—I found that the critical step to facilitating a family's participation in the funeral liturgy is an immediate visit to the survivors home upon learning of a death. The people present are usually and quite understandably filled with all types of emotions—shock, grief, anger, confusion, doubts, worry, and guilt. For the priest just to be there at that initial time, to listen and to empathize, is in itself an invaluable pastoral ministry. Sometimes he will be asked to assist the stricken family members with some practical tasks or needed decisions.

Eventually I gently try to turn their attention to the funeral liturgy, bringing with me a twenty-five minute video, Death and Life, and a booklet, Through Death to Life. The video first describes the funeral Mass and then outlines ways in which the family can participate. The latter repeats those possibilities, but also includes the many options for prayers, readings, and blessings available in the ritual and a tear-out selection form. I leave both items with the family.

In their troubled condition, family members often hardly hear what I am saying. I reassure them that the vigil service or wake and funeral Mass will in themselves be a great source of comfort, understanding, and strength, even if they choose not to take an active role in their preparation and celebration. I also tell them that after things settle down a bit, they may wish to watch the film and glance at the booklet. I mention that those who do engage in helping prepare the liturgical celebrations tend to find that it actually helps them cope with their loss and grief. Nevertheless, if they choose not to get involved in either the preparing or participating as ministers, this is certainly acceptable.

Before leaving, we work out a time, usually before or after calling hours, when I can visit with them about specific details of the funeral Mass. In my experience, most families, once the initial trauma has subsided somewhat, will at least pick up the booklet and make several selections. Others will become more deeply involved, using most of the alternatives listed below.

Practical Possibilities

- *Passages from the Bible:* The funeral rite lists more than seventy scripture readings available for a funeral service with or without a Mass. The booklet Through Death to Life contains all of them. The surviving family members may select three: one from the Old Testament, one from the New Testament, and one from the gospels. Or they may select two: one from either the Old or New Testament and one from the gospels. They may also wish to ask family members, relatives or friends to read the Old and New Testament passages at the service. The priest or deacon proclaims the gospel reading that the family members have chosen.

- *Funeral Homily*: The priest or deacon will give a brief homily based on the family's choice of the scripture readings. While it is not meant to be any kind of eulogy, the homilist will nevertheless find it helpful to speak beforehand with some family members about the deceased's life so he can better integrate those particular texts and the reasons for their selections into his message.

- *Prayers and Blessings*: There are also numerous prayers and blessings such as forty-eight Opening Prayers from which loved ones can choose a favorite.

- *Music*: Very often the family working with the parish musician selects appropriate songs or other melodies that speak to them of the deceased and of their belief in the resurrection.

- *General Intercessions or Prayers for the Faithful*: The Order of Christian Funerals includes nine samples. The family may use any one of these formulas, combine parts of several, adapt the intentions provided, or compose petitions that are entirely their own. If they create their own, the petitions should express the congregation's prayerful concern for others in the world. These would naturally include the deceased and the bereaved and should also reach out to persons in the local, national, and global communities who are in need of support.

- *Participation Booklets*: Many parishes today work with the family to develop leaflets, also personalized, which will assist persons who participate in the service itself.

- *Placing of the Pall*: A funeral pall, reminding us of the garment given at baptism and therefore symbolizing our life in Christ, is draped over the coffin at the beginning of the liturgy. Family members or friends are encouraged to do this, although the priest or another minister of the service may likewise do the placing of the pall. The use of this pall also signifies that all are equal in the eyes of God (James 2:1–9) and that baptism opens for us the gates of heaven.

- *Placing of Christian Symbols*: A symbol of the Christian life may be carried in the procession by a family member or friend and placed on the coffin when it is finally situated before the altar. This may be a bible or book of the gospels as a sign that Christians live by the word of God and that fidelity to that word leads to eternal life. It might also be a cross as a sign that the Christian is marked by the cross in baptism and that through Jesus' suffering on the cross is brought to the victory of his resurrection. The priest may recite a prayer to accompany this placing of the symbol on the coffin.

- *Presentation of Gifts*: The Catholic Church encourages family members or friends at the Funeral Mass to bring the bread and wine to the altar. In addition, they may also wish to bring to the church beforehand some gifts symbolic of their beloved's life and place them on a small table in front of or near the altar. While the arrangement of these symbols is not part of the liturgy, for many their presence as part of the prayer environment says in effect, "Lord, we give our loved one back to you." The following items have been used in past funerals to express symbolically the main interests, loves, and efforts of the deceased person: a wedding photo, a family portrait, a familiar rosary, crucifix, and prayer book, a carpenter's hammer, a saxophone player's sheet music, a nurse's cap, a certificate of appreciation for service given upon retirement.

- *Words of Remembrance:* Following the Prayer after Communion and before the Final Commendation, a member or friend of the family may speak in remembrance of the deceased. This is an occasion to cite some of the ways in which the departed has inspired us and deepened our faith through her or his life on earth. These remarks ideally should be relatively brief, limited to three persons at a maximum and written in advance.

- *Personalized Memorial Cards*: The family usually decides on some standard memorial cards, or, as in the case of the family in our introductory story, design their own for distribution during calling hours, at the funeral and in later appreciation or acknowledgment notes.

- *Communication with the Presiding Minister*: Family members need to share with the presiding priest or deacon the various choices and decisions they have made about the above elements of the liturgical celebrations. They should also express additional desires they have or any questions or concerns they need to have addressed. The selection form in the back of Through Death to Life, for example, can facilitate that. This will help the presiding minister prepare a funeral service that will have a personal touch to it and reflect the family's needs and wishes.

Bereavement Committees

More and more Catholic churches have a committee or group of parishioners who assist with the funeral preparations, music, and a luncheon, as well as subsequently minister to the family in any number of ways. One committee might immediately visit the home, fulfill the tasks that we have described the priest performing earlier in this chapter, and share this information with the one who is to preside at the service. A second group consists of a small funeral choir for the liturgy.

A third arranges a luncheon for the bereaved family and friends following the funeral.

A fourth group sends cards or calls upon the grieving members for a period of time afterwards.

In a variety of ways, the contemporary *Order of Christian Funerals* by itself brings great comfort, understanding, and strength to the bereaved. When family members and loved ones actually plan the funeral liturgy and actively participate in it, this ritual does so in an even more powerful way.

nine

Eternity

Sergeant Mark, twenty-two years old and stationed in Germany, had been gravely injured in a car accident and for two days was being sustained by life-support machines. However, his brain functions ceased, and his loved ones and doctors decided to unhook the machines. Several persons gathered around the bedside for those final moments. They included three doctors, his closest friend Danny—a 6'5" soldier—Danny's wife Patty, Mark's commanding officer, and a Catholic priest.

The priest led them through prayers for the dying and then added an Our Father and a few Hail Marys. During these petitions Danny clutched his wife with one hand and Marks' inert hand with the other. As the doctors turned valves and halted the machines, Danny put his head on Mark's chest and cried. When the process was over, Danny stopped crying, stood up straight and pounded Mark's chest. With a loud and strong voice, he declared:

"Sergeant Mark, congratulations! You are the first of all of us to make it home! Goodbye!"

Home means eternity, heaven, and everlasting life. The cover of *Newsweek's* August 12, 2002, issue featured a medieval artist's image of heaven and the title of its main article: "Visions of Heaven." I was surprised to learn from their poll that 76 percent of Americans believe in heaven and 71 percent think it's an actual place. However, after that remarkable agreement, the views of heaven move in totally different directions.

Father William Shannon, long-time member of the religious studies department at Nazareth College in Rochester and a great student of the late Thomas Merton, reminds us in his book, *Here on the Way to There*, that heaven, like God, is totally beyond our human comprehension. He writes:

But, as we reflect more on heaven and the imagery we use to clarify it, we realize in the end that heaven will always far exceed any and all the realities and experiences that our age or any other age in history has or will draw on to try to say what heaven really is. Try as we may, heaven's beauty is simply beyond all telling. There is nothing in our human experience that can adequately mirror the wonders of heaven. Heaven, when achieved, will always be a surprise!

With that caution in mind, I would like to give a brief and rather traditional description of what we believe about heaven. This sketch is based upon biblical and liturgical texts, the most current official Catholic teaching, and illustrations or applications taken from several popular contemporary novels.

In the Presence of God

Heaven, paradise, or eternity means that we stand in glory before the presence of God and see God face to face, not through faith or grace as upon earth. John's first letter promises this as our destiny:

Beloved, we are God's children now; what we shall be has not yet been revealed. We do know that when it is revealed we shall be like him, for we shall see him as he is (1 Jn 3:2).

Eucharistic Prayer III of the Mass reflects that prediction in this special petition for a deceased person:

There we hope to share in your glory
when every tear will be wiped away.
On that day we shall see you, our God, as you are.
We shall become like you and praise you forever
through Christ our Lord, from whom all good things
come.

The Catechism of the Catholic Church likewise echoes John's teaching:

Those who die in God's grace and friendship and are perfectly purified live forever with Christ. They are like God forever, for they "see him as he is," face to face (CCC, #1023).

The Church calls that contemplation of God in heavenly glory the beatific vision. This beatific vision, in which God is revealed in an inexhaustible way to all those in heaven, becomes "the ever-flowing well-spring of happiness, peace, and mutual communion" (CCC, #1045). This essential element of heaven may not immediately sound emotionally thrilling or powerfully inspirational. However, a short reflection should make it so.

Saint Augustine (d. 430) proclaimed this now famous phrase: "You have made us for yourself, and our hearts are restless until they rest in you." Human experiences testify to the truth of his assertion.

• Those who pray consistently and seriously may occasionally receive passing glimpses of God and fleeting tastes of the divine. A consequent longing for the fullness of being in God's presence will certainly motivate such people.

• Human beings deep down seek for the eternal, the timeless, the permanent. They know that vacations end, jobs terminate, and relationships sometimes waver. The promised notion of close personal connections lasting forever can surely be comforting and inspiring, for example, to a couple married for many years who contemplate their eventual deaths and separations in this world.

- We likewise yearn for perfect happiness. While there are moments of great joy here on earth, we also know times of deep sorrow as well. We can be up and down, elated and depressed; peaceful and content at some periods, but agitated and worried at others.

Cast in light of those reflections, meeting God face to face, together with the permanently and perfectly satisfying happiness flowing from that experience, should be attractive and alluring indeed.

In Alice Sebold's popular novel *The Lovely Bones*, an older man attacks a fourteen-year-old girl, ravages her, and murders her. Many never are able to move beyond the first chapter in which the story of this horrible event is told. The rest of the book, however, follows the young woman in heaven, observing the lives of her family, friends, and murderer. At one point she describes her experience in heaven and captures this first element of eternity—being in God's presence: "I would like to tell you that it is beautiful here, that I am, you will one day be, forever safe."

Reunited with Loved Ones

As the time of Jesus' passion and death drew near, a certain heaviness descended upon his followers. Christ then reassured them, urging those disciples not to be troubled, but to have faith. He also promised a future home in which they would be together again.

> In my Father's house there are many dwelling places. If there were not, would I have told you that I am going to prepare a place for you? And if I go and

prepare a place for you, I will come back again and take you to myself, so that where I am you also may be (Jn 14:23).

One option for the "Prayer of Commendation" at the funeral rite's conclusion includes this phrase:

Merciful Lord,
turn toward us and listen to our prayers:
open the gates of paradise to your servant
and help us who remain
to comfort one another with assurances of faith,
until we all meet in Christ
and are with you and with our brother / sister for ever.
—*Order of Christian Funerals*, #175–A

The Catechism declares that Christ has opened heaven to all who believe in him.

He makes partners in his heavenly glorification those who have believed in him and remain faithful to his will. Heaven is the blessed community of all who are perfectly incorporated into Christ (CCC, #1026).

This enormously comforting prospect of being reunited with our loved ones must have special meaning for those anticipating or experiencing the death of a beloved.

I have often witnessed how the possibility of eventual reunion sustains the bereaved. At a special Mass in November for the peace of all those who had died during the previous year and for the consolation of their survivors, both Jim and Charles were present. Jim's wife of many decades died months after a long struggle with cancer, and Charles' six-month-old daughter expired suddenly and unexpectedly. They both no doubt uttered the same words: "I miss her terribly and long for the time I will see her again."

Sports commentator Mitch Albom, whose *Tuesdays With Morrie* was and continues to be a national bestseller, subsequently wrote the novel *The Five People You Meet In Heaven*. His introductory dedication for this tale of fiction, however, is to a real uncle who gave Albom his first concept of heaven:

> Every year, around the Thanksgiving table, he spoke of a night in the hospital when he awoke to see the souls of the departed loved ones sitting on the edge of the bed, waiting for him. I never forgot that story. And I never forgot him.

End of All Suffering

The final section of the Book of Revelation contains a description of "a new heaven and a new earth." It announces that God will be with the chosen people always and "will wipe away every tear from their eyes, and there shall be no more death or mourning, wailing or pain, for the old order has passed away" (Rv. 21:3–4). The *Order of Christian Funerals* offers this passage as one of the options for the first reading at the Funeral Mass. It also provides forty-seven "Prayers for the Dead" that can be used in various parts of the funeral rites, including the opening prayer. One of them contains these words:

> The old order has passed away: welcome him/her then into paradise, where there will be no sorrow, no weeping nor pain, but the fullness of peace and joy with your Son and the Holy Spirit for ever and ever (#398-4).

When a person encounters a very serious illness, the family and the sick individual usually begin praying intensely for a healing, a miracle, and a restoration to health. When the condition deteriorates, clearly becomes terminal, and painful suffering ensues, the petitions tend to slowly change. "God, please take her/him" and "Please take me" are not uncommon requests.

Such pleading may initially cause inner conflict for those praying. However, in most cases that tension slowly dissipates and gradually moves toward a sense of surrender, of letting go. The suffering is just too much to endure or to observe.

The vision of no more tears, sorrow, or pain in heaven must be reassuring and consoling for both the dying individual and those caregivers who are surrounding the desperately ill person with love. In *The Five People You Meet in Heaven*, Albom recounts the experience of Eddie, an older amusement park caretaker, who enters heaven after a fatal accident.

> Where is my worry? Where is my pain? Every hurt he'd ever suffered, every ache he'd ever endured— it was gone as an expired breath. He could not feel agony. He could not feel sadness . . . he felt no fear.

Earth and Heaven Connect

In the Second Book of Maccabees, Judas discovered that his fallen soldiers had been wearing a forbidden pagan amulet. Troubled by their religious defection, he took up a collection among his troops to send to Jerusalem for a sacrifice in the temple so that these sins might be blotted out. The following Old Testament text makes this commentary about Judas' action:

> In doing this he acted in a very excellent and noble way, inasmuch as he had the resurrection of the dead in view; for if he were not expecting the fallen to rise again, it would have been useless and foolish to pray for them in death. But if he did this with a view to the splendid reward that awaits those who have gone to their rest in godliness, it was a holy and pious thought.

> —*2 Maccabees* 12:38–45

Every Sunday, Catholics stand and recite the Nicene Creed, concluding with the sentence, "We look for the resurrection of the dead, and the life of the world to come."

Moreover, every Eucharistic Prayer includes an intercession on behalf of the dead. Eucharistic Prayer II, for example, phrases that petition in this way:

Remember our brothers and sisters
who have gone to their rest
in the hope of rising again;
bring them and all the departed
into the light of your presence.

—Eucharistic Prayer II

All of the Eucharistic Prayers also plead that we will one day join the saints in heaven.

In talking about the communion of heaven and earth, the Catechism draws on this teaching from Lumen gentium (LG), the Dogmatic Constitution on the Church, from the Second Vatican Council:

Being more closely united to Christ, those who dwell in heaven fix the whole Church more firmly in holiness. . . . They do not cease to intercede with the Father for us, as they proffer the merits which they acquired on earth through the one mediator between God and men, Christ Jesus. . . . So by their fraternal concern is our weakness greatly helped (LG, #49).

The saints themselves teach us about the joining of heaven and earth. Saint Dominic (d. 1221) spoke these words to members of his community when he was dying: "Do not weep, for I shall be more useful to you after my death and I shall help you then more effectively than during my dying life." And Saint Therese of Lisieux, the Little Flower, (1873–1897) proclaimed: "I want to spend my heaven in doing good on earth" (CCC, #956).

As Catholic Christians we have countless times repeated those words, "the communion of saints," prayed for persons who have died, and asked for help from those already in heaven. However, over the past quarter century, the spiritual or mystical connection between those in the next world and us here on earth has become more personal and intimate for many people. This shift may have begun in connection with the 1975 publication of Doctor Raymond A. Moody's groundbreaking book, *Life After Life*. His description of various survivals after bodily death prompted many similar stories from people who described their perceptions during near-death experiences as brief glimpses at the life to come.

In *When the Dying Speak*, Ron Wooten-Green, a university professor, Catholic lay minister, and hospice chaplain, shared numerous instances in which terminally ill people spoke to him of their perceived encounters with those who had died. It seems to me that today more and more people on earth feel a caring link with those they have loved who are now in the next life. In *Charming Billy*, novelist Alice McDermott reflects this faith in a close link between those in heaven and those on earth. The lead character in that book recalls a conversation between her mother, dying of cancer, and her father:

> It made it easier that they both believed in the simplest kind of afterlife—that my father could say to her, even in those last days, joking but without irony, "You're going to get tired of hearing from me. I'll be asking you for this that and the other thing twenty-four hours a day. Jesus, you'll be saying, here comes another prayer from Dennis." And my mother would reply, her voice hoarse with pain, "Jesus might advise you to take in a movie once in a while. Give your poor wife a rest. She's in heaven after all" (p. 45).

Nicholas Sparks also dramatizes such a connection in his novel *The Guardian*. Jules, a widow at only twenty-five, was grieving on Christmas Eve over the loss of her husband but forty days earlier. The doorbell rang and a young man delivered a package to her with the instructions not to shake the carton and keep one end up. He said that she would understand once the gift had been opened. Inside was a puppy, a Great Dane who would become her guardian, together with a letter from her husband obviously written prior to his death. The note concluded:

> And don't worry. From wherever I am, I'll watch out for you. I'll be your guardian angel, sweetheart. You can count on me to keep you safe. I love you (p. xii).

Deathless Love

Sullivan Ballou, a young Providence lawyer with a promising political career, enlisted in the army at the outbreak of the Civil War. From a camp near Washington, he wrote a letter to his wife Sarah and spoke of his "deathless love" for her. Aware that he soon might perish in battle, Ballou reassured her:

> O Sarah! If the dead can come back to this earth and flit unseen around those they loved, I shall always be near you; in the gladdest days and darkest nights . . . always, always. Sarah, do not mourn me dead; think I am gone and wait for thee, for we shall meet again (p. 84).

ten

Those Left Behind

Popular novelist Nicholas Sparks experienced three terribly difficult family deaths: his mother at an early age through a horse-riding fall, his father some years later in a car accident, and his only sister Dana, who succumbed to cancer when she was but thirty-three years old. The author describes in his book, Three Weeks with My Brother, *how after Dana's death, Sparks suddenly became more aware of life and the preciousness of time:*

> *I came to believe that because life could end at any moment, I had to be prepared for any eventuality. I wanted to make sure my family was taken care of, no matter what might happen in the future. I had goals, and with the clock ticking, I had to hurry up and meet them before the unthinkable occurred. There was suddenly no time to waste (p. 340).*

People often asked Nicholas and his brother Micah how they continue to function, even flourish in the face of much tragedy in their lives. The novelist responds:

> *I can't answer that question, except to say that neither Micah nor I ever considered the alternative. We'd been raised to survive, to meet challenges, and to chase our dreams (pp. 354–355).*

Highly respected author Joan Didion wrote The Year of Magical Thinking *after her husband of forty years died suddenly through a massive coronary. That traumatic event was intensified by the concurrent serious illness of their only young daughter Quintana. She gives the rationale behind her book:*

> *This is my attempt to make sense of the period that followed, weeks and then months that cut loose any fixed idea*

> *I had ever had about death, about illness, about probability and luck, about good fortune and bad, about marriage and children and memory, about grief, about ways in which people do and do not deal with the fact that life ends, about the shallowness of sanity, about life itself (p. 7).*

Later Didion comments on the grieving process:

> *We are imperfect mortal beings, aware of that mortality even as we push it away, failed by our very own complication, so wired that when we mourn our losses we also mourn, for better or for worse, ourselves. As we were. As we are no longer. As we will one day not be at all (p.198).*

Death and Dying

Dr. Elizabeth Kubler-Ross, a Chicago psychiatrist, wrote *On Death and Dying* in 1969, a text that soon became a classic reference work on the subject. Her research with terminally ill patients revealed that these persons generally pass through five stages in their last weeks, days, and hours. Moreover, such varying feelings, moods, or attitudes often, in fact usually, occur also among members of the sick person's family and those close to the critically ill patient. Nevertheless, these others may experience the stages quite differently from the terminally infirm individuals.

Those stages or conditions are neither chronological nor stable, nor always present. Patients (and their caregivers) do not necessarily move from the first through each to the last. They may likewise go back and forth, in and out of different moods. Finally, desperately sick patients sometimes skip one stage or another, and never reach the final attitude of acceptance.

It should be noted that these five stages or attitudes can be found at times among people who are experiencing or have experienced any deep personal loss. That includes not only those who grieve over the death of someone they love, but also persons who have lost their jobs, good health, homes through a natural disaster, or spouses because of marital disruption or divorce. The five stages, attitudes, or feelings are:

Denial: The prospect of a major loss is so frightening and overwhelming that some deny either its reality or even its possibility.

Anger: When confronted with this painful event beyond their control, others may feel irritated or angry and strike out at someone or something, including God. When such annoyance is directed toward the Lord, the situation becomes more complicated. The anger can then turn into confusion, regret, or remorse for this turning against the Creator.

Bargaining: Still others occasionally make a bargain, usually with God and ordinarily for a specific period of time. "I will go back to church on a regular basis if I live to see my child graduate." These bargaining arrangements are generally a very secret exchange between the petitioner and the Lord.

Depression: The sad feelings that accompany depression arise from someone looking backwards—blaming himself or herself for what is happening and feeling guilty, as well as lamenting the loss of valued parts of their lives like family, job, and friends. Those feelings may also surface from a look forward—the impending separation from this life on earth and from those we love, together with an uncertainty about the future.

Acceptance: In *The Gift of Peace*, Joseph Cardinal Bernardin described battles with two bouts of cancer. The final one led to his death. Surrendering or simply letting go was a key attitude that brought him great serenity and peace.

Some critically ill persons sense, realize, or welcome the fact that their pain will soon be over and the struggle finished. They wait with resignation and acceptance for the final journey into eternity. Caregivers and family members as well as those coping with other types of losses may also experience an acceptance, but of a different nature.

Waves

When a large ship passes, it creates a series of waves that are relatively huge and close together. As the boat moves on, the waves subside somewhat both in size and frequency. Experienced ocean swimmers by the shore have learned the skill of diving through such massive waves. There is a certain daring courage in this process—plunging into the base of the wave at precisely the right time, then hearing or feeling the crash of that wave hitting a sandy bottom just beyond the swimmer's feet. These water veterans know that the waves will subside and they will quickly surface, able to breathe again. However, those unfamiliar with the ocean may panic, fear they will drown, and frantically flail their arms in attempts to reach the surface. Those futile efforts can cause them to be roughly thrown to the ocean floor by the powerful waves and even lead to more disastrous developments. There is a parallel between such seashore experiences and the process of coping with grief after a personal loss.

Dealing with Feelings

Those five stages, attitudes, or feelings that Elizabeth Kubler-Ross identified are essentially emotions, which are by nature undulating or wave-like; they ebb and flow, come and go. Often they begin in one's gut or stomach and then rise to the top of one's head. People who understand the wave-like nature of feelings such as sadness and loneliness that accompany grief simply let these emotions wash over them. They know that soon enough these feelings will eventually subside even though they are now quite intense. That awareness does not necessarily eliminate or even diminish the pain. Still the knowledge that the emotion is a temporary experience helps the afflicted person remain relatively calm, more serene and certainly hopeful.

People who do not understand this wave-like nature of feelings generally find them more painful. The sadness or loneliness, for example, engulfs them, drowns them, and throws them off balance. They think the pain will never end. Sometimes in their darkness they may flail in a futile way to dispel the negative feelings, longing for someone or something to rescue them. Those frantic efforts usually make matters worse and can even cause tragic consequences.

Two Illustrations

Mary, an upstate New York mother in her sixties, was informed by a police officer that her thirty-eight-year-old son had been stabbed to death in New York City's Central Park. Several hours later I visited the stunned mother. Family and friends surrounded her in her home. However, Mary just sat immobile in her chair, staring out the window. I sat down next to her, held her hand, and later, spoke about the five stages and waves of grief. She made no response at all, but continued her stoic gaze straight ahead. I said to myself, "That was a dumb thing to do, a purely academic lecture." I left Mary's side and spent perhaps fifteen minutes with those gathered in the house. Suddenly the distraught, silent woman uttered a few soft words. When I returned to her, she simply said: "I am feeling a wave."

Jane recently learned that after many years and countless procedures, she had, through the marvels of modern medical science, become pregnant for the first time. About a month later, however, another announcement, also the product of the latest medical techniques, dampened the joy and elation, mixing the feelings with sadness and worry. She had a disease, currently incurable, that would slowly cause the deterioration of her entire body. We visited for a lengthy period of time, and I described the stages and the waves. She responded: "In a single hour I have experienced all those feelings. My stomach and whole being has been like a spaghetti bowl of emotions, churning swiftly from one stage to another."

The ship and wave analogy holds true in these circumstances as well. In the beginning, the waves are huge and frequent, reaching the shore very close together, almost indistinguishable. As the vessel moves farther away, the waves diminish in size and frequency, becoming more distinguishable. When the loss is sudden and unexpected, like in both of the above examples, the stages, attitudes, and feelings often are compressed together much as Jane described them—a churning "spaghetti bowl." As the news and reality sink in, the emotions gradually tend to separate out and surface in different ways and at different moments. In all those situations, understanding the wave-like nature of stages or emotions seems to make them more bearable.

An Onion

In the days of vinyl record albums, before CDs, the needle sometimes lodged in a particular groove and the words or music would keep repeating over and over again. The needle, stuck in one spot, never moved on, never went forward. A parallel exists for some who are grieving. They seemingly cannot move on or go forward. Usually, however, a grieving person eventually recognizes that it is time to do so. Otherwise, mourning can turn into a self-pity that does not allow for growth and a new beginning. There is, however, no chronological order or precise moment when that happens, nor will the healing ever be complete and the sense of loss disappear.

The analogy of an onion can be helpful here. When one peels off a layer of the onion, the sharp odor can bring tears. But then it seems to lose its potency. Nevertheless, by peeling off another layer, it regains its strength and causes tears again. So it is also with grief and mourning. Consider the following experience.

Patricia's husband died much like Joan Didion's spouse—a sudden coronary leaving her a widow with several young children. One year later she asked to speak with me. Patricia thought that now, nearly a year later, she should be over her loss. But a holiday, an anniversary date, or a particular song on the radio seemed to trigger tears or a rush of temporary sadness. Was she losing her mind, the woman inquired? Not at all. Each event was simply like peeling off another layer of the onion. Those experiences, although to a lesser degree, will probably continue for the rest of her life. They are signs of both her love and her loss. That is but one example why words like "Time will heal" or "You will get over this" are neither very helpful, or comforting, nor even accurate.

Moving On

Still, there does come a moment when grieving persons often say to themselves: "I am slipping into self-pity, feeling sorry for myself. It is time for me to dry my tears and move on. The person I loved so much and miss so badly would not want me to carry on in this way." Again, an example or two could prove of value.

The university professor came home as usual for lunch with his wife, a woman who had been suffering from serious depression. She did not greet him in the customary way; in fact she could not be found in the house. He finally looked into the garage and found her slumped over the wheel of their car. The suicide, while not totally unexpected, was still a shock and devastating to this man. The professor now recalls that in the days and months following her death, he often retold the details of his coming home, searching and finding her. The very telling of the experience seemed to help in his grieving process. But eventually the man realized that the time had come not to repeat the story, but to dry his tears and move on.

In Nicholas Sparks' novel *The Guardian*, which I cited in the last chapter, Jim, in that letter to his wife, Jules, likewise urges her to move on:

> It would break my heart if I thought you'd never be happy again. So please do that for me. Be happy again. Find someone who makes you happy. It might be hard, you might not think it's possible, but I'd like you to try. The world is a better place when you smile (p. xii).

Hope for the Future

I would like to conclude this chapter and this little book with a word of hope for the future directed particularly to those grieving the loss of someone or several who have left or soon will leave our world for the next. That, of course, means most of us.

The first word of hope comes from Sullivan Ballou, whom you met in the last chapter. He actually died in the battle of Bull Run one month after he wrote that touching letter to his "very dear Sarah." In his note he urges her: "Do not mourn me dead; think I am gone and wait for thee, for we shall meet again."

The other word of hope is also a repeat from the last chapter. Jesus gave to his disciples and to us this promise: "And if I go and prepare a place for you, I will come back again and take you to myself, so that where I am you also may be" (Jn 14:3).

Those indeed are comforting messages of hope for all of us as we prepare for eternity.

Acknowledgments

Every author knows that any book requires the assistance and input of many people. I wish to acknowledge with deep gratitude these persons who made this work possible:

- The energetic, visionary pastor and dedicated, efficient pastoral care director of San Antonio Roman Catholic Church in Port Charlotte, Florida. Their concern about misunderstandings over "the last rites" prompted the expansion of my response to their question into this small book.

- Mr. Robert Hamma and Ms. Eileen Ponder of Ave Maria Press, who liked my proposal, sought reactions to the initial outline from a number of people in pastoral ministry, and then, guided by that input, approved with recommendations the project and directed the completed manuscript through the necessary editorial stages.

- Cynthia Heath, Elaine and Steve Jacobs, Dr. Joel Potash, Ann and Sam Buranich, the late Father Kevin Murphy, that forty-year-old nameless man who wrote of his liberating reconciliation experience, the dying house painter, Frank Fatti and his family, the late sergeant Mark with his closest friend soldier Danny, and finally, Nicholas Sparks and Joan Didion—all for their real-life stories that began these chapters.

- The other persons whose experiences I have described in these pages, but whose names and circumstances have been altered for privacy's sake.

- Peter Dwyer, long time friend and director of Liturgical Press in Collegeville, who was supportive of this as he has been of my many projects.

- The authors of those many resources included in this book, both the professional texts and contemporary novels.

- Those people who read the manuscript and responded with encouragement and support as well as, in some cases, with very helpful comments that have improved this book: Ann and Sam Buranich, Dan Cantone, Cindy Falise, Frank and Pat Fatti, Elaine and Steve Jacobs, Patricia Livingston, Vincent Nicolia, David Pasinski, James Philips, Pauline Russell, Fathers Don Krebs, John Roark, Ronald Rohlheiser, Tom Zedar, and Monsignor Michael Ryan.

- Bishop Thomas J. Costello, a friend for over sixty years and also a very skilled editor, who greatly improved the text and ensured that my words were faithful to Catholic teaching.

- Mrs. Ann Tyndall, my administrative assistant, nurse, and friend, who with difficulty converted a handwritten text into a readable, computerized document and who, together with her spouse, Dr. Gary Tyndall, also my friend and physician for over a decade, at the same time guided me through the first six months of semiretirement and those health care issues that accompany seventy-five years of age, a fractured wrist and the treatable, but incurable bone-marrow cancer called Waldenstrom's Disease.

Resources

The resources noted here were very helpful in providing insights, stories, and quotations for the chapters indicated:

Chapter 1 Making A Will
Daniel G. Cantone, Attorney and Counselor at Law.

Chapter 2 End-of-life Issues
Time, December 12, 2005, p.58.

Catechism of the Catholic Church (United States Conference of Catholic Bishops, 1997), #2278–2279.

National Conference of Catholic Bishops. *Ethical and Religious Directives for Catholic Health Care Services* (United States Catholic Conference #029–X, 1971, 2001), #57–59. Quoted in *Living With Grief: Ethical Dilemmas of Life* (Hospice Foundation of America, 2005).

Richard McCormick, 1997, Quote also taken from *Living with Grief*, p. 51.

Pope John Paul II, *Life-Sustaining Treatments and Vegetative State: Scientific Advances and Ethical Dilemmas*, March 20, 2004. Quoted in *Ethics and Medics*, November 2005 (National Catholic Bioethics Center), p. 1.

Living With Grief, p. 28 (see above for full reference).

"Letters to Editor," *Commonweal*, April 22, 2005, p. 2.

David E. Pasinski, "Voices," *Syracuse Catholic Sun*, April 28–May 4, 2005, p. 2.

Australian Catholic Bishops Conference, *Briefing Note On the Obligation to Provide Nutrition and Hydration*, 2004, concluding paragraph.

Chapter 3 Health Care Proxies and Organ Donations

Dr. Joel Potash, Center for Bioethics and Humanities, SUNY Upstate Medical University, Syracuse.

Advanced Care Planning: Compassion and Support at the End of Life. Excellus Blue Cross Blue Shield Company, Rochester, New York. Published with permission of Partnership for Caring, Inc., Washington, D.C.

Catechism of the Catholic Church, #2296.

Anatomical Gift Program, Upstate Medical University, State University of New York, Syracuse.

Chapter 4 Cremation

"Cremation" from *Order of Christian Funerals* with *Cremation Rite.* (International Committee on English in the Liturgy, Inc., 1989, 1985), #413–415, 417.

Chapter 5 Postponing Eternity

Francis McNutt, *Healing* (Ave Maria Press), 1974, 1999.

"General Introduction" and "Anointing Outside Mass" of *Pastoral Care of Sick,* (International Committee on English in the Liturgy, Inc.,1982), #6, 8–14, 25, 125A.

Chapter 6 Heart Light as a Feather

Karl Menninger, *Whatever Became of Sin?* (Hawthorn, 1973).

Chapter 7 Last Rites

"Celebration of Viaticum" in *Pastoral Care of the Sick* (International Committee on English in the Liturgy, Inc., 1982), #175, 181.

Joseph Champlin and Susan Champlin Taylor, *A Thoughtful Word, A Healing Touch* (Twenty-Third Publications, 1995), pp. 25–27.

Chapter 8 A Comforting Farewell

"General Introduction" of *Order of Christian Funerals* (International Committee on English in the Liturgy, Inc., 1989, 1985), #17.

Joseph Champlin, *Through Death to Life* (Ave Maria Press, 2002).

Chapter 9 Eternity

Story of Sergeant Mark by Ronald Rolheiser in *Forgotten Among the Lilies* (Doubleday, 2005), pp. 286–288.

Newsweek, August 12, 2002, cover and feature story.

William Shannon, *Here on the Way to There: A Catholic Perspective on Dying and What Follows* (St. Anthony Messenger Press, 2005), p. 116.

Eucharistic Prayers III and II of *The Roman Missal*.

Catechism of the Catholic Church, #1023, 1026, 956.

Robert Ellsberg, *All Saints* (Crossroads, 1997), pp. 370–372 (reference to St. Augustine).

Alice Sebold, *The Lovely Bones* (Little Brown, 2002), p. 324.

"Funeral Mass" and "Prayers for the Dead" of *Order of Christian Funerals* (International Committee on English in the Liturgy, Inc., 1989, 1985), #175–A, 398–4.

Mitch Albom, *The Five People You Meet in Heaven* (Hyperion, 2003), pp. 21–22.

Raymond A. Moody, *Life After Life* (Bantam Books, 2001).

Ron Wooten-Green, *When the Dying Speak* (Loyola Press, 2002).

Alice McDermott, *Charming Billy* (Dell Publishing, 1999), p. 45.

Nicholas Sparks, *The Guardian* (Warner Books, 2004), p. xii.

Joseph Champlin, *Slow Down* (Ave Maria Press, 2004), Day 42, p. 84.

Chapter 10 Those Left Behind

Nicholas and Micah Sparks, *Three Weeks With My Brother* (Warner Books, 2004), pp. 340, 354–355.

Joan Didion, *The Year of Magical Thinking* (Knopf, 2005), pp. 7, 198.

Elizabeth Kubler-Ross, *On Death and Dying* (Scribner, 1997).

Joseph Cardinal Bernadin, *Gift of Peace* (Loyola Press, 1997).

Nicholas Sparks, *The Guardian* (Warner Books, 2004), p. xii.

William Bennett, *The Moral Compass* (Simon and Schuster, 1995), pp. 578–579.

Father Joseph M. Champlin serves in sacramental ministry as resident priest at Our Lady of Counsel in Warners, New York. He is former rector of the Cathedral of the Immaculate Conception in his home diocese of Syracuse. A prolific writer on a variety of pastoral care and spirituality concerns, he is also a regular featured guest on *Seize the Day with Gus Lloyd*, a show that airs on Sirius Radio channel 159.

Fr. Champlin has traveled more than two million miles lecturing in the United States and abroad. Among his more than fifty books are: *Slow Down* and *Take Five* (Sorin Books), *Should We Marry?*, *From the Heart*, *Together for Life*, and *Through Death to Life* (Ave Maria Press).

Also by Fr. Champlin